D1220971

189056

PRIMARY SOURCES IN AMERICAN HISTORY™

THE FRENCH AND INDIAN WAR

A PRIMARY SOURCE HISTORY OF THE FIGHT FOR TERRITORY IN NORTH AMERICA

CAROLYN GARD

rosen central

Primary Source™

The Rosen Publishing Group, Inc., New York

GRAND ISLAND PUBLIC LIBRARY

Published in 2004 by The Rosen Publishing Group, Inc.
29 East 21st Street, New York, NY 10010

Copyright © 2004 by The Rosen Publishing Group, Inc.

First Edition

All rights reserved. No part of this book may be reproduced in any form without permission in writing from the publisher, except by a reviewer.

Library of Congress Cataloging-in-Publication Data

Gard, Carolyn.
The French Indian War: a primary source history of the fight for territory in North America / by Carolyn Gard.— 1st ed.
  p. cm. — (Primary sources in American history)
Includes bibliographical references and index.
Contents: Washington goes to Ohio, 1754—British and French engagements, 1755—The French advance, 1756 and 1757—The British begin winning, 1758—The decisive battle of Quebec, 1759.
ISBN 0-8239-4511-1 (library binding)
1. United States—History—French and Indian War, 1755–1763—Juvenile literature. [1. United States—History—French and Indian War, 1755–1763.] I. Title. II. Series.
E199.G17 2003
973.2'6—dc21

2003010683

Manufactured in the United States of America

On the front cover: *Defeating Braddock*, a 1755 oil painting by an unknown artist.

On the back cover: First row *(left to right)*: committee drafting the Declaration of Independence for action by the Continental Congress; Edward Braddock and troops ambushed by Indians at Fort Duquesne. Second row *(left to right)*: the Mayflower in Plymouth Harbor; the Oregon Trail at Barlow Cutoff. Third row *(left to right)*: slaves waiting at a slave market; the USS *Chesapeake* under fire from the HMS *Shannon*.

CONTENTS

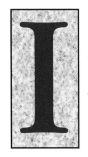

INTRODUCTION

During the 1700s, wars between Great Britain and France erupted with some frequency. Three of these wars had to do with succession—who would rule what country—in Europe. The fourth war, called the Seven Years' War or the French and Indian War, was different because it was about control of territory. It was also unique because it started not in Europe, but in North America.

The early French and British colonizers in North America ran into few conflicts with each other because the ways they settled the country differed. The British colonies spread out along the eastern seacoast, stretching from Maine down to the Carolinas, but they were blocked on the west by the 1,000-mile-long Allegheny Mountains.

VALUABLE TERRITORY

French trappers penetrated the interior by taking boats up the Saint Lawrence River and into the Great Lakes. Settlements followed. By the 1750s, French colonists lived on both sides of the waterways, from Quebec, Canada, to Detroit.

A third group that played an important role in the French and Indian War was, of course, the Indians. For about 200 years, five tribes in what is now New York State—the Mohawks, the Oneidas, the Onandagas, the Cayugas, and the Senecas—had been united as the Five Nations of the Iroquois. This group protected others who

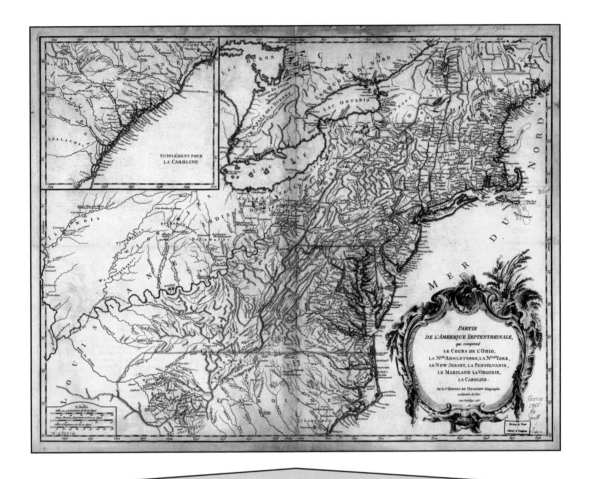

This 1755 hand-colored map by Gilles Robert de Vaugondy (1688–1766), "mapmaker to the king," shows portions of North America that were established at the time of the French and Indian War. England controlled the states on the coast, from New England to the Carolinas. France controlled the interior. Both countries realized they needed to claim the land and waters that led to the important Mississippi River.

wanted to join them. However, any tribe that did not want to join became an enemy. The Iroquois chased their enemies west, gaining a reputation as fierce warriors. In 1750, the members of the Five Nations numbered about 10,000 people living in fifty villages.

As North America was settled, these three groups were bound to clash. The Indians wanted the trade goods they could get from the Europeans, particularly guns and ammunition to make them even fiercer warriors. Both France and Britain tried to persuade the Iroquois to make an alliance with them. In the end, the war chiefs elected to stand with the British. In turn, the British supplied them with arms and encouraged them to attack French settlements in the Great Lakes area and the Ohio River Valley.

Not to be outmaneuvered, the French made alliances with the Algonquian-speaking Indians (including the Delaware, Miami, Ojibwa, Ottawa, Pottawatomi, Shawnee, and Huron tribes) who lived along the Saint Lawrence and the Great Lakes. Some of these tribes had been chased to the west by the Iroquois. The French acted as mediators among the various Indian groups to unite them in their hatred of the Iroquois. Whether the tribes were allied with the French or the British, the Indians had similar goals—to prevent either the British or the French from gaining dominance in the Ohio Valley.

In the 1750s, about 55,000 French colonists lived in Canada and 1,000,000 British lived along the Atlantic coast. As their settlements grew, both the British and the French looked west to the Ohio Valley. The French wanted to control the Ohio River to facilitate travel between their settlements in Canada and those in the Mississippi River Valley. They saw these rivers as the key to trade and travel throughout the interior of the country. The British wanted the Ohio Valley for its trade value. They also knew they could make fortunes from sales of the land.

Both countries asserted rights to the Ohio Valley. Britain claimed all the land from 34° to 45° latitude (North Carolina to

Nova Scotia) and "to the west indefinitely." France claimed the interior lands, which it named New France, on the grounds that French explorers such as La Salle and Louis Joliet had been the first to "discover" these lands. To complicate matters, the Iroquois also claimed the territory by right of prior occupation.

In 1749, the Ohio Company, a group of British land speculators, began building forts and selling land in the Ohio Valley to farmers despite French demands that the British leave the area. In 1752, French soldiers led a group of Algonquian warriors in an attack on Pickawillany, the largest British settlement and the richest trading post in the area. The raid sent many British settlers fleeing back across the mountains.

The new governor-general of New France, the marquis de Duquesne, arrived in Quebec in July of 1752. Duquesne, a man of action rather than diplomacy, ordered that four forts be built in the Ohio Country as a show of France's military strength.

The lieutenant governor of the influential colony of Virginia, Robert Dinwiddie, recognized the seriousness of the crisis. Dinwiddie wrote to the Board of Trade in London asking for instructions on ridding the Ohio Country of the French. The board wrote back: "You are warranted by the king's instructions to repel any hostile attempt by force of arms . . . You have now his majesty's orders, for erecting forts within the king's own territory. If you are interrupted therein, those who presume to prevent you from putting into execution, an order, which his majesty has an undoubted, (nay, hitherto and undisputed) right to give, are the aggressors and commit an hostile act."

The situation had become a powder keg waiting to explode.

TIMELINE

May 28, 1754 — War begins with George Washington's defeat of the French and the establishment of Fort Necessity.

June 14, 1754 — An English-Iroquois trade conference is held in Albany, New York, to prevent breakup of their alliance.

July 3, 1754 — The French take Fort Necessity.

February 23, 1755 — General Edward Braddock arrives in the colonies from England and takes command of British forces in North America.

July 8, 1755 — The French defeat General Edward Braddock's forces near Fort Duquesne, and Braddock is mortally wounded.

September 9, 1755 — The British win the Battle of Lake George.

May 18–19, 1756 — Great Britain and France declare war on each other.

August 14, 1756 — French forces under Lieutenant General Joseph-Louis Montcalm capture Fort Oswego.

TIMELINE

August 1757 — The British abandon plans to capture Fort Louisbourg.

August 9, 1757 — Montcalm takes Fort William Henry.

July 26, 1758 — The British take Fort Louisbourg. The French fleet in Canada is destroyed.

October 21, 1758 — The British make peace with the Iroquois, Shawnee, and Delaware Indians.

November 24, 1758 — The French destroy Fort Duquesne and flee ahead of the British assault.

July 26, 1759 — The British take Fort Carillon on Lake Champlain.

September 13, 1759 — In the Battle of Quebec, both Montcalm and Major General James Wolfe are killed.

May 11–16, 1760 — The French siege of Quebec fails.

February 10, 1763 — The end of the war. The Treaty of Paris gives all of France's possessions east of the Mississippi (except for New Orleans) to England.

CHAPTER 1

In 1753, Governor Robert Dinwiddie of Virginia learned that the French had built two forts on the south shore of Lake Erie. The governor commissioned twenty-one-year-old George Washington to deliver a letter to the French commandant at Fort Le Boeuf on Lake Erie ordering the French to leave the area. While Dinwiddie's approach was somewhat idealistic, it was a safe choice: Since he didn't have enough forces to physically remove the French, he had to try a diplomatic approach.

WASHINGTON GOES TO OHIO

One of the major reasons for wanting to get the French out was to prevent them from building a fort at the place where the Monongahela and Allegheny Rivers come together to form the Ohio River (today, Pittsburgh, Pennsylvania, sits at this point). Such a fort would not only be a strategic defensive position in the heart of

For this 1772 Charles Willson Peale portrait, George Washington was represented as he looked nearly twenty years earlier, when he served in the French and Indian War. His part in the war brought young Washington recognition, and he went on to play a key role in the Revolutionary War and then to become the first president of the United States of America. The character trait largely responsible for Washington's success was his courage: He claimed he was unable to fear anything or anyone.

the Ohio Valley, it would also be a symbol of power. The country that controlled this location could limit the expansion of others.

Washington's Journey

Washington left Williamsburg, Virginia, on October 31, 1753, with Dinwiddie's letter in hand. Three weeks later, Washington, his guide, and his interpreter arrived at the forks of the Ohio and set up camp. Washington surveyed the area, concluding that the land between the Monongahela and the Allegheny was the best place for a fort. In late November 1753, he wrote in his journal about the location: "[I]t has the absolute Command of both Rivers . . . well-timbered Land all around it, very convenient for building."

While at this spot, Washington sought out the local Indian chiefs to persuade them to remain loyal to the British cause. After three days of negotiation with various Indian leaders including Tanaghrisson, the Seneca chief, who was also known as the Half-King, Tanaghrisson agreed to accompany Washington north to Fort Le Boeuf near Lake Erie. The chief promised to order the French to leave.

On December 11, the weary group arrived at Fort Le Boeuf, having endured mud, freezing rain, and snow. Washington presented Governor Dinwiddie's letter to Captain Saint-Pierre, the commander of Fort Le Boeuf. Dinwiddie had written: "The Lands upon the Ohio River are so notoriously known to be the property of the Crown of Great Britain that it is a matter of equal concern and surprise to me, to hear that a body of French forces are erecting fortresses and making settlements upon that river, within his Majesty's domain. I must desire You to acquaint me by whose Authority and Instructions You have lately marcht from

Canada with an arm'd Force, & Invaded the King of Great Britain's Territories . . . it becomes my Duty to require your peaceable departure."

On December 14, Saint-Pierre handed Washington his reply to Dinwiddie. Not surprisingly, it read in part: "As to the summons you sent me to retire, I do not think myself obliged to obey it."

Building Forts on the Forks

On his return to Williamsburg, on January 16, 1754, Washington was promoted to the rank of lieutenant colonel and given another commission. He was to take 200 men to the forks of the Ohio to defend the interests of Virginia. Fur trader William Trent would go ahead with a group of carpenters to build a fort at that location to be called Fort Prince George.

With the help of the nearby Indians, the carpenters began work on the fort. On April 18, 1754, French captain Pierre de Contrecoeur and a force of 600 troops took the partially completed stockade by force from the 40 Virginians. The French demolished that fort and built a bigger and better one that boasted a parade ground, a guardhouse, officers' quarters, supply and powder magazines, a hospital, a blacksmith shop, and a bakery. The French named the post Fort Duquesne.

Back in Virginia, Washington was able to raise only 160 untrained and poorly equipped troops. Anxious to keep the fort from falling into French hands, he pushed ahead with his troops instead of waiting for reinforcements.

On May 24, when Washington was about sixty miles away from the forks, he heard of the surrender at Fort Duquesne. He fell back to a location called Great Meadows in order to prepare for an attack. On May 28, the British troops surprised an advance

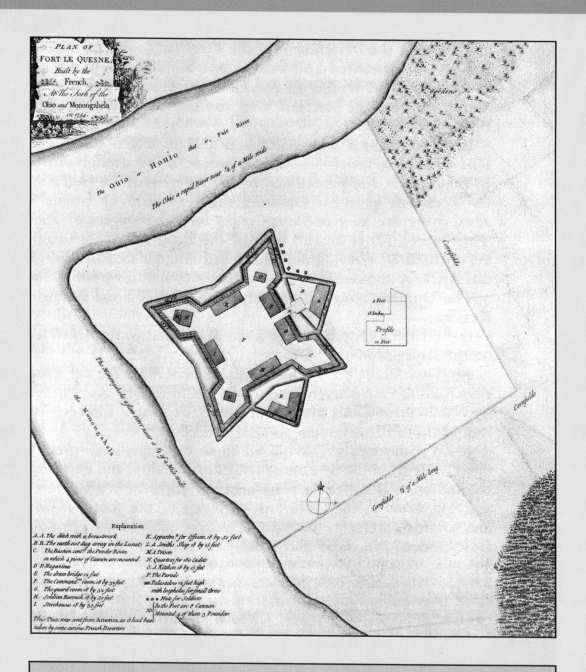

PLAN OF
FORT LE QUESNE.
Built by the
French,
At The Fork of the
Ohio and Monongahela
in 1754.

The OHIO or HOHIO that is Fair River

The Ohio a rapid River near ¼ of a Mile wide

Gardens

Cornfields

The Monongahela a Mile wide

The Monongahela a swift river near at ¼ of a Mile wide

Profile

Cornfields

Cornfields ¼ of a Mile long

Explanation

A.A. The ditch with a breastwork
B.B. The earth not dug away in the Lunets
C. The Bastion contd the Powder Room
    on which 4 pieces of Cannon are mounted
D D Magazines
E The draw bridge 12 feet
F. The Command room 18 by 32 feet
G. The guard room 18 by 32 feet
H. Soldiers Barrack 18 by 50 feet
I Storehouse 18 by 35 feet

K Appartms for Officers 18 by 50 feet
L A Smiths Shop 18 by 15 feet
M A Prison
N Quarters for 180 Cadets
O A Kitchen 18 by 15 feet
P The Parade
▬ Palasadoes 12 feet high
    with loopholes for small Arms
▪▪▪ Hut for Soldiers
✸ In the Fort are 8 Cannon
    Mounted 4 of them 3 Pounders

This Plan was sent from America, as it had been
taken by some curious French Deserters

J. Payne created this plan of Fort Duquesne as it appeared in 1754. It was published in London, England, in 1756 as part of a broadside and is now in the Library of Congress. The sketch shows the fort situated at the fork of the Ohio (called the "Fair River" in the plan) and the Monongahela Rivers. Both rivers are marked as being one-quarter mile wide. The "explanation" at the lower left corner lists parts of the fort such as the magazine, drawbridge, prison, kitchen, and soldiers' huts. Below the key it is noted, "This Plan was sent from America, as it had been taken by some curious French Deserters."

group of French scouts. The attack ended with the murder of one of the French commanders, Ensign Jumonville.

Reinforcements arrived, bringing the number of men with Washington to 400. The British set about building a fort at Great Meadows, which they named Fort Necessity. Washington's attempts to persuade the Indians to join the British failed. Tanaghrisson realized that the Indians had nothing to gain by helping the British control and settle the Ohio Valley.

Despite the lack of Indian support, Washington worked on improving the road and transporting artillery to Fort Duquesne. On June 28, he received word that a force of more than 700 men and 350 Indians had left Fort Duquesne headed for Great Meadows. Wisely, Washington took his exhausted men back to Fort Necessity.

The Indian Alliance

In June 1754, the Board of Trade in London, the group that oversaw the American colonies, ordered Lieutenant Governor James DeLancey of New York to convene a meeting in Albany. The governor invited representatives from the other British colonies and Indians from the Five Nations to come together to discuss how to get the colonies to work together for the common defense and to ensure that the Indians stayed loyal to Britain. This was called the Albany Plan.

Benjamin Franklin, a delegate from Pennsylvania, pushed for the colonies to cooperate. To emphasize his goal, he made a woodcut of a rattlesnake cut into parts, each part labeled as one of the colonies. Under the snake were the words "Join, or Die." The congress adopted the Albany Plan, but when the delegates took it back home their legislatures rejected it.

Benjamin Franklin's famous 1754 cartoon "Join, or Die" shows sections of a snake representing the American colonies. The sections are labeled South Carolina, North Carolina, Virginia, Maryland, Pennsylvania, New Jersey, New York, and New England. Together the pieces formed a whole, but if even one colony chose not to participate, the snake wouldn't survive. Although created to unite the colonies against Indians in the 1750s, the woodcut went on to became a symbol during America's revolutionary activity of the 1770s.

The Indians presented the conference with some of their grievances. One of them had to do with the fur trade. When the Albany merchants figured out that they were the only people to whom the Indians could sell their furs, the merchants cheated the Indians by paying such small sums for the furs that the Indians could not buy many trade goods. The

Indians also complained that they had received miserly presents and that the British were encroaching on their land. (In fact, at the conference some of the delegates offered the Indians liquor until they sold their land to the colonies.) The Indians asked that William Johnson, a man they trusted, be put in charge of Indian affairs.

Chief Hendrick of the Mohawks warned the conference, "[Y]ou have neglected us for these three years past. You have thus thrown us behind your back; whereas the French are a subtle and vigilant people, always using their utmost endeavors to seduce and bring us over to them." The delegates had no power to grant the Indians' requests, but they promised to consider all the demands.

The Loss of Fort Necessity

On July 3, the French attacked Fort Necessity. Washington wrote in his diary about the misery of the day.

[The French] then, from every little rising, tree, stump, stone, and bush kept up a constant galding fire upon us; which was returned in the best manner we could till late in the afternoon when their fell the most tremendous rain that can be conceived, filled our trenches with water, wet, not only the ammunition in the cartoosh boxes and fire locks, but that which was in a small temporary stockade in the middle of the entrenchment called Fort Necessity erected for the sole purpose of its security, and that of the few stores we had; and left us with nothing but a few (for all were not provided with them) bayonets for defense. In this situation and no prospect of bettering it, terms of

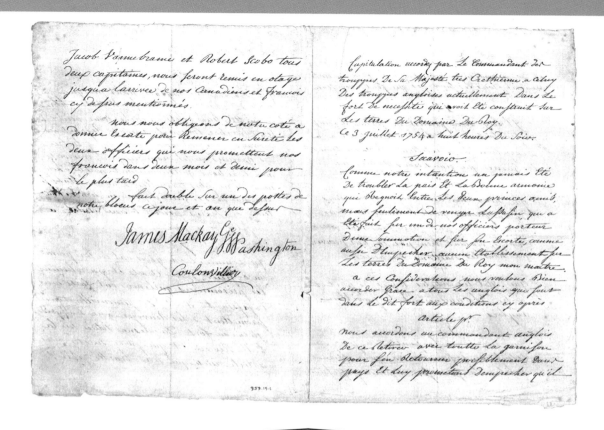

George Washington signed the article of capitulation *(above)* on July 3, 1754, when he and British officer James Mackay surrendered Fort Necessity to the French. See transcription on pages 56–57. Written in French, the document refers to the death of Jumonville as an assassination. Washington never admitted the killing was an assassination. He claimed he signed the document based on his translator's use of the words "loss" and "death" instead. The capitulation is housed in the Royal Ontario Museum in Toronto, Canada.

capitulation were offered to us by the French which with some alterations that were insisted upon were the more readily acceded to, as we had no salt provisions, and but indifferently supplied with fresh, which from the heat of the weather would not keep; and because a full third of our numbers, officers as well as privates were, by this time, killed or wounded.

The British were overwhelmed by the French forces, as well as by the weather. Out of food, and with many of their men dead, they surrendered.

Washington signed the letters of capitulation, taking full responsibility for the death of Jumonville. Two of the British officers offered themselves as hostages. This was to be of some benefit later, as one of them, Captain Stobo, managed to smuggle the plans for Fort Duquesne to the British.

Thirty British troops were killed, while the French lost only three men. As the British painfully made their way home, the French destroyed Fort Necessity. When Washington arrived in Williamsburg, the Virginia Council blamed him for the failure. Washington resigned his commission.

Historians consider the attack on Fort Necessity as the first battle of the French and Indian War.

CHAPTER 2

BRITISH AND FRENCH ENGAGEMENTS

After hearing of Washington's defeat, the officials in London realized that they had to stop the French if they were to keep their North American territories. King George II of Britain approved sending two regiments of Irish infantry to America led by Major General Edward Braddock. Braddock arrived in Virginia in February 1755. His 1,000 troops with guns and supplies landed three weeks later.

The French were not to be outdone. On hearing of the British reinforcements, France sent 3,000 troops to America under the command of Major General Jean-Armand Dieskau. The British sent warships to intercept this fleet and prevent it from landing in Canada, but a thick fog allowed them to capture only three of the French ships.

Edward Braddock (1695–1755) was appointed commander in chief of all British forces in North America. After Braddock lost his life at the disastrous battle at Fort Duquesne, George Washington wrote of him "Thus died a man, whose good and bad qualities were intimately blended. He was brave even to a fault and in regular Service would have done honor to his profession. His attachments were warm, his enmities were strong, and having no disguise about him, both appeared in full force."

GEN. BRADDOCK.

Braddock's Plan

Braddock proposed a four-pronged military plan to the colonies. William Johnson would lead forces to take Fort Frederic at Crown Point on Lake Champlain. This was a crucial position, since the passage through Lake Champlain and on to the Hudson River was the easiest way for forces to move from Canada to New York. For the safety of their colonies, the British needed to control this access.

Braddock himself would lead a second group to recapture Fort Duquesne. The third group would destroy Fort Beausejour in what is now Nova Scotia at the mouth of the Saint Lawrence River, thus blocking access to the interior by the French fleet. A fourth group under William Shirley, the governor of Massachusetts, would capture Fort Niagara.

The March to Fort Duquesne

On June 16, British forces captured Fort Beausejour in Nova Scotia. Meanwhile, Braddock was making preparations to march to Fort Duquesne, more than 100 miles away through trackless wilderness over mountains, an incredible challenge. The entourage had 1,445 regular soldiers, 262 provincials in independent companies, 30 sailors to work the block and tackle to move the cannon over the mountains, 449 other troops, 8 Indian scouts, 10 six- and twelve-pound guns, 4 howitzers [cannons], and 14 small mortars. In addition, they had to carry shot, shells, powder, and food for the men and their horses. Only after Benjamin Franklin used his powers of persuasion on the local farmers was the expedition able to get enough wagons and horses to transport the provisions. George Washington went along as an unpaid volunteer.

This plan illustrates Braddock's advance party as it made its way to Fort Duquesne on the morning of July 9, 1755. An advance guard paving the way through the woods was followed by the main body, which included Braddock and his staff, 500 troops, and artillery. The column was secured on either side by multiple groupings of soldiers. This highly organized unit turned to chaos once the French and their Indian allies ambushed them.

Braddock thought he could capture Fort Duquesne without the help of Indian scouts and fighters. He disliked everything about the Indians and felt his European fighting tactics could be successful in the Ohio wilderness. When the Indians offered to help, Braddock told them bluntly that they would not be allowed to remain in the Ohio Valley. The chiefs responded, according to Francis Jenning's book *Empire of Fortune*, "That if they might not have Liberty to Live on the Land they would not fight for it." At this point, most of them dispersed, either going back to their villages or joining the French at Fort Duquesne.

Braddock assembled his troops at Fort Cumberland on the Potomac River in Maryland, about 100 miles from Fort Duquesne, while he waited for supplies, wagons, and horses. On June 10, the group left Fort Cumberland. They made barely three miles a day since they had to hack out a twelve-foot-wide road, blast rocks, and build bridges over swamps and streams. The servant of one of the captains in an advance party wrote in his journal:

Thursday May the 29th. This day we marched about seven miles and was 8 hours of marching it, it being very Bad Roads that we Where Oblig'd to halt Every hundred yards and mend them. As soon as we Came to our [encampment] ground there was a working party sent out to Cut the Roads, and a Covering party to guide them, the Working party Being 200 men, the Covering party 100.

Fryday May the 30th. We marched at 6 oClock. The party that Cut the roads marched at four. We marched till Eight at Night and only marched three miles.

Parts of this road became the Mason-Dixon Line, which later separated the slave states and the free states.

A Second Defeat at the Forks

Scouts reported that French reinforcements had headed to Fort Duquesne. On the dubious advice of Washington, Braddock separated his forces, taking a quick strike group ahead and leaving the heavier equipment and most of the supplies to come at a slower pace. Even with this lighter load, the group took nineteen days to march 100 miles.

On July 8, Braddock's troops closed to within nine miles of Fort Duquesne only to be ambushed by the French and their Indian allies. As the British troops marched forward in columns, the French and Indians shot at them from behind bushes and rocks. The French gradually moved back to surround the main British forces. The British forces panicked and ran to the rear where the units mixed together in confusion.

Braddock had four horses shot out from under him. After three hours of futile attempts to dislodge the French, he ordered a retreat. Throughout that night, the remnants of Braddock's group plunged through the woods, intent on finding the supply wagons. According to the diary of one of the British officers, "In making the road we [had] marked the trees on each side of it, which we found of very great Use to us in our retreat, for being obliged to keep marching the whole night through a continued Wood, the people frequently lost their way, & had nothing to put them right except feeling for the Marks."

Two days later, the fleeing group met the supply wagons, and the men ate their first real meal in several days. They didn't have enough horses to transport the supplies and ammunition back

DEFEAT OF GENERAL BRADDOCK, IN THE FRENCH AND INDIAN WAR, IN VIRGINIA, IN 1755.

Edward Braddock's gruesome death is captured in the engraving shown above. *Defeat of General Braddock, in the French and Indian War, in Virginia, in 1755,* shows the ambush from the perspective of the Indians who hid in the woods and pounced on Braddock's party. Although the French and their Indian allies were outnumbered, they overcame the British by hiding behind trees and taking careful and accurate aim at their opponents. The 1855 engraving is housed in the Library of Congress.

to Fort Cumberland, but they couldn't just leave them for the French. Instead, they destroyed the mortars, buried the shot, and burned the rest, including the wagons and the provisions they couldn't carry.

Braddock had been mortally wounded in the battle. He died on July 13, 1755, with the words, "Who would have thought it? We shall better know how to deal with them another time." The men buried him on the road and then marched over his grave to obliterate any signs of the resting place. Five days later, they arrived at Fort Cumberland, completely demoralized.

The Remaining Attacks

In late summer, William Johnson led 3,500 untrained troops up the Hudson River Valley to the point where he had to portage by carrying boats across the land. There he constructed Fort Edward as a supply base. As the men worked on Fort Edward, the French commander in Quebec, Major General Dieskau, heard of Johnson's movements. If the French were to retain control of the links to their western forts, he had to stop the British advance. Instead of waiting for the British to besiege Fort Frederic on Lake Champlain, Dieskau decided to surprise Johnson's troops.

On September 7, Mohawk scouts warned Johnson of Dieskau's approach. Leaving troops to defend Fort Edward, Johnson set out with 1,600 men to meet Dieskau. Johnson formed his troops into a semicircle on the road with each side anchored on the lake. They piled up wagons, barrels, logs, and boats to form barriers. The French and their Indian allies could only attack in two directions and were unable to stand against the British fire.

When William Shirley heard of Braddock's defeat in August, he decided that Fort Oswego, which he planned to use as a supply base, could not be defended. Instead of going on to Fort Niagara, Shirley left 700 men to repair Fort Oswego over the winter and returned to Massachusetts.

As the winter of 1755–1756 approached, the forces rested and made plans for the next season's campaigns.

CHAPTER 3

In 1756, both the British and the French governments emphasized the importance of the war in North America by sending new commanders in chief to the colonies. The new French commander, Lieutenant General Louis-Joseph Montcalm, arrived in North America in May 1756. The British earl of Loudoun reached North America in July. By this time, the home governments of Britain and France admitted that they were actually at war. On May 18, 1756, Great Britain declared war on France. The next day France returned the gesture.

THE FRENCH ADVANCE

The Loss of Fort Oswego

Meanwhile, the garrison that had been left to repair Fort Oswego on Lake Ontario fought scurvy and starvation. With the lakes and rivers frozen, supplies couldn't get through. Spring opened the waters, but it also brought out French and Indian raiders. In March the French ambushed one supply train; a second train managed to reach the fort only to be ambushed on the return trip. Despite constant Indian raids, the fort commander, Lieutenant Colonel Mercer, hoped that they could defend the British outpost on the Great Lakes.

Montcalm had other plans for the fort. On July 21, he left Quebec with 3,000 men and a number of Indians to capture Fort

Engraved for the London Magazine, 1760.

A South View of OSWEGO, on Lake Ontario, in North America.

Explanation
1 The River Onondago
2 Lake Ontario

Fort Oswego was a British fort built in 1726. It is shown above in an engraving, circa 1760, that was originally published in *London Magazine*. The body of water in the foreground is the Onondaga River. It flows into Lake Ontario, which is in the background. Although the fort was captured for France by Montcalm, it was reoccupied by the British and later passed to the United States.

Oswego. The location of the fort had been badly chosen—between two hills where cannon fire could easily reach it. On August 12, Montcalm opened siege. The French built a parapet and platforms from which they could fire directly into the fort. On August 13, they took nearby Fort Ontario. Mercer was killed, and his second in command, Lieutenant Colonel John Littlehales, surrendered Fort Oswego.

After the surrender of Fort Oswego, Montcalm wrote to Brigadier General Francois Gaston de Levis: "I am master of the three forts of Chouegen [Oswego] which I demolish[ed]: of 1,600 prisoners, five flags, one hundred guns, three military chests, victuals for two years, six armed sloops, two hundred bateaux and an astonishing booty made by our Canadians and Indians. All this cost us only thirty men killed and wounded." With the loss of Fort Oswego came the loss of British control over Lake Ontario.

The Ranger Forces

Although the British lacked the number of Indian allies that the French had, they had a formidable force in their rangers. Rangers were soldiers who were skilled in fighting Indians and working in the wilderness. Governor William Shirley described the duties of the rangers in a July 26, 1756, letter to Henry Fox, saying that they were "to try to intercept the Enemy's Convoy's of Provisions and Stores upon Lake Champlain and to make Discovery of their Strength and Motions."

Throughout the winter of 1756–1757, Captain Robert Rogers and his rangers patrolled the woods around Lakes George and Champlain, harassing the French and the Indians. They used skates and snowshoes for the winter travel.

The rangers learned that Montcalm intended to attack Fort William Henry. This fort, the base for British action against New France, posed an unacceptable threat to the French. Although the French had moved most of their troops back to Montreal, leaving only a token garrison at each fort, the British didn't attack but retired to their winter quarters in New York, Boston, and Philadelphia.

Robert Rogers is portrayed in this 1776 engraving wearing full military gear, posing in a wooded area, with watchful Indians in the background. Rogers and his rangers helped the British immensely in the French and Indian War by using fighting strategies of the Indians themselves, such as surprise, stealth, and ambush. Rogers' Rangers are considered to be the precursor to today's special operations unit, the Army Rangers.

Fort Louisbourg Remains French

Back in London, William Pitt became the prime minister. Pitt didn't just want to defeat France—he wanted to conquer New France. This could be accomplished by cutting off French access to the Saint Lawrence River. Canada needed the military supplies, grain, and trade goods that came from France. If the British, with their superior navy, blockaded the river, Canada could not survive.

The key to Pitt's plan was to capture the fortress of Louisbourg on Cape Breton Island near the mouth of the Saint Lawrence River. French ships used the fort as a refitting station before making their transatlantic voyages. On June 20, 1757, Loudoun sailed for Fort Louisbourg with more than 100 ships carrying 6,000 troops. By the time Loudoun arrived near Louisbourg and met the Royal Navy squadron, the French had three squadrons sitting in Louisbourg harbor and 3,000 troops in the fort. After consulting with the British admiral on August 4, Loudoun decided that victory was not possible, and he sailed back to New York.

The Surrender of Fort William Henry

While Loudoun sat with his troops in the Louisbourg harbor, the French assembled 6,000 troops at Fort Carillon on Lake Champlain as well as 2,000 Indians. By contrast, the British had only 1,500 men at Fort William Henry. The French took advantage of the diminished defenses in New York. On August 2, they began the siege of Fort William Henry.

The French brought their heavy artillery within a half mile of the fort. Once the batteries were in place, the French began a

Painted by Thomas Davies (1737–1812), this painting shows what is believed to be a ranger at work. Created in 1759, it is the only known period illustration of a ranger in action. In the painting's background are the lines at Lake George. Sitting on the ground is most likely a Stockbridge Indian Ranger.

five-day bombardment of the fort. On August 7, Montcalm's aide-de-camp, Louis de Bougainville, wrote in his journal,

> At nine in the morning after a double salvo from the right and left batteries, the Marquis de Montcalm sent me to carry to the fort's commander the letter of General Webb which was intercepted on the fifth. I walked out of the trenches with a red flag carried before me [the French flag was white, so flags of truce were red], accompanied by a drummer beating his drum and in escort of fifteen grenadiers.

Bougainville was blindfolded and taken into the fort. He delivered his letter, and then was blindfolded again as he was led out.

By August 9, the fort had been heavily damaged; only five cannons were operable, and the ammunition was nearly gone. The commander of Fort William Henry surrendered.

Montcalm's terms of surrender followed the European pattern. In return for the British troops promising not to fight for eighteen months, they would be given safe passage to Fort Edward. The French would care for the wounded, all prisoners would be returned, and the soldiers would be allowed to keep their personal effects.

Unfortunately, these terms were alien to Montcalm's Indian allies. The Indians were in this fight for plunder and captives, as promised by the French, and these they were determined to get. The Indians entered the fort, killed many of the wounded, and plundered the troops waiting to be evacuated. The next morning, as the British began to march to Fort Edward, the Indians set upon them,

In this 1761 illustration of the siege of Fort William Henry, French soldiers and Indian warriors scalp the British troops they took prisoner. The image appeared in a book called *The Cruel Massacre of the Protestants in North-America: Shewing How the French and Indians Joined Together to Scalp the English, and the Manner of their Scalping*, which was published in England to further turn the public against France. The truth was that British soldiers, too, were guilty of scalping their enemies.

killing many, stripping them of their possessions, and taking women and children captive. By the time the French restored order, 185 soldiers had been killed, and 300 to 500 were taken as captives.

Although the attack on Fort William Henry was a victory for France, its Indian allies, who had played key roles in many of the battles, now turned against the French. The Indians felt that Montcalm had deceived them. Never again would the French be able to gather such an Indian force. Montcalm had also alienated the British. Should the British gain the upper hand, he knew they would not offer the honors of war to his troops.

CHAPTER 4

After enduring two years of disastrous losses, William Pitt relieved Loudoun of his command and made some other major changes. The British navy would stop French ships from resupplying their troops in Canada and give the British colonists the chance to defeat the French defenders.

Another of Pitt's strategies was to get more help and more manpower from the colonies by making them partners with London and by offering incentives to the recruits. In December 1757, Pitt wrote to the governors of Massachusetts Bay, New Hampshire, Connecticut, Rhode Island, New York, and New Jersey: "I am commanded . . . that you do forthwith use your utmost Endeavours, and Influence with the council and Assembly of your Province, to induce them to Raise, with all possible Dispatch, as large a Body of Men within your Government, as the Numbers of its Inhabitants may allow . . . And the better to facilitate this service the King is pleased to leave it to you to issue commission to such Gentlemen of your Province." Pitt also promised that all provincial officers would have the same rank as their counterparts in the regular army, and

THE BRITISH BEGIN WINNING

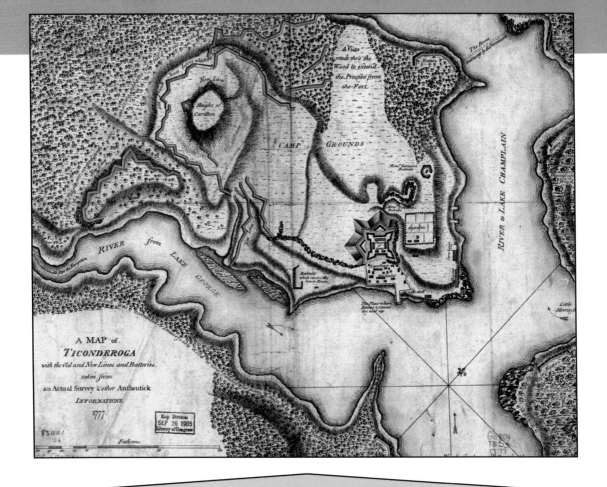

This map shows Ticonderoga and the French Fort Carillon as it was set up at the time of its attack. The area was desirable because it controlled the English-claimed Hudson River and the French-claimed St. Lawrence River. Bordered by waterways ("Ticonderoga" is Iroquois for "place between two waters") and with a heavily fortified land entrance, the fort proved difficult to take. After a humiliating defeat in July 1758, the British captured the fort in 1759.

they would be furnished with arms, ammunition, and tents. The colonies showed their support for these new ideas by quickly recruiting enough volunteers to fill the regiments. The British cause had new energy.

New Strategies

Pitt's plans for 1758 were to capture Fort Louisbourg, to capture Fort Carillon on Lake Champlain, and to attack Fort Duquesne. These three forts were the keys to mounting a successful invasion of Canada and to cutting off the supplies to the French colonies. Pitt backed up his plans by sending more troops and money to America.

Somewhat optimistically, the *Boston Gazette* announced the plan to capture Louisbourg and then all of Canada on March 29, 1758:

> The good Time is at Length arrived, when we may retrieve the Mistakes we have committed in the Conduct of the present War. We have endeavoured at an immense Charge, only to lop the Branches, without laying Ax to the Root of the Tree. A united and vigorous Attempt upon Canada has been long desir'd and expected, as the best Method to decide the Contest between us and our perfidious Enemies . . . Canada must be destroyed.

Success at Fort Louisbourg

By June 1758, the British were ready to march on Fort Louisbourg. Major General Jeffrey Amherst amassed a force of 11,000 men. The troops, traveling aboard ships under the command of Admiral Boscawen, arrived in Cape Breton on June 2, where 3,000 French troops defended Fort Louisbourg. After capturing Lighthouse Point, the British began a siege of the fort. The French held out for forty-nine days of bombardment before surrendering on July 26. In revenge for the massacre at Fort William Henry, Amherst allowed the French no honors. Anyone who had taken up arms against the British was made a prisoner of war. The 8,000 men, women, and children who lived on Cape Breton Island were deported to France.

Not only did the British take Fort Louisbourg, but their 157 warships wiped out the French fleet, a crippling blow to the French.

While Amherst savored the first British victory in two years, Major General James Abercromby gathered 6,300 troops and 5,900 provincials at the ruins of Fort William Henry. Their goal was to take Fort Carillon and cut off France's access to the British colonies. They were joined by Rogers' Rangers, who had spent the previous winter scouting out the area.

A Lopsided Fort Carillon Defeat

Brigadier Lord Howe—according to Major General James Wolfe, "the best soldier in the British army"—was put in charge of the army. On July 5, he led 16,000 troops onto 1,000 small boats to begin their "march" up Lake George to Ticonderoga, a piece of land sticking out into Lake Champlain that held the French Fort Carillon. The British flotilla covered the lake from side to side for a distance of seven miles. Four miles from Fort Carillon, the troops landed and began an overland march. They routed the French advance camp, but in the pursuit Howe was killed. This loss of the commander led to mass confusion among the troops. Many of the men retreated to the landing place, and the British lost their advantage.

Abercromby camped about an hour away from Ticonderoga, where he waited for reinforcements to arrive. This delay played into the hands of Montcalm, the commander of Fort Carillon, whose 3,500 troops were outnumbered by the British. While the British waited, the French brought in more troops and constructed defensive works.

The French built a wall of logs with holes for guns and topped it with sandbags. Below the wall, they made a maze of

The portrait of George Augustus, Viscount Howe (1722–1758) was painted in the eighteenth century. Howe's death on the way to Ticonderoga brought chaos to the British troops. Howe's brothers were important military men as well: Richard (1726–1799) was commander of British naval forces in North America from 1776 to 1778. William (1729–1814) was commander in chief of the British army in North America from 1775 to 1778. The William L. Clements Library at the University of Michigan boasts a collection of the Howe brothers' papers.

logs with sharpened branches, an early version of today's concertina wire. The attackers got tangled in this maze and were easy targets.

Abercromby decided to storm the breastworks without using artillery. The British attacked in their well-disciplined ranks. As the troops entered the maze, the straight lines broke up, giving the French ample opportunity to fire at them. Major Eyre, an engineer who was acting as the commander of the 44th Regiment, wrote in a July 1758 letter to the surgeon James Napier:

Trees were fell down in Such Manner that it Broke our Batallions before we got near the Breastwork. All [that] was left for each Commanding Officer of 'A Reg[iment] to do, was to support & march up as quick as they could get Upon their Ground And so on to the Intrenchm[en]t.

Another survivor recalled:

Our orders were to [run] to the breast work and get in if we could. But their lines were full, and they killed our men so fast, that we could not gain it. We got behind trees, logs, and stumps, and covered ourselves as we could from the enemy's fire … A man could not stand erect without being hit, any more than he could stand out in a shower, without having drops of rain fall upon him; for the balls came by handsfull.

Abercromby, seeing that he had lost some 2,000 troops, retreated to Fort William Henry, where they built a fortified camp. Abercromby received much criticism for retreating from forces that were a quarter the size of his.

Fort Duquesne Abandoned

The third strategy, the attack on Fort Duquesne, got under way in late July with Brigadier General John Forbes commanding 6,000 troops. Forbes knew that the Indians had played an important role in Braddock's failed attack on Fort Duquesne in 1755, and he wanted their support. To do this, he enlisted the help of Moravian minister Christian Frederik Post. In October, after a nineteen-day council, the Iroquois, Shawnee, and Delaware refused to help the French defend Fort Duquesne in return for the British promise that all lands west of the Alleghenies would remain Indian.

The Indians gave Post a message to take back to the British: "That all the nations had jointly agreed to defend their hunting place at Alleghenny and suffer nobody to settle there; and as these Indians are very much inclined to the English interest, so he begged us very much to tell the Governor, General, and all other people not to settle there." Post agreed to take the message back, but he doubted that anyone would listen.

The French sensed defeat. When Forbes and his 2,500 men arrived at Fort Duquesne on November 25, they found the French gone, the fort blown up, and the storehouses burned. Forbes expressed his happiness over the ease of this victory in a letter to Abercromby on November 26, 1758. Forbes wrote,

> I have the Pleasure of Acquainting you with signall success of His Majesties Arms over all his Enemies on the Ohio, by having obliged them to burn and abandon their Fort of Duquesne ... The Enemy having made their escape down the river, part in boats and part by land to their forts and settlements on the Mississippi, being abandoned, or at least not seconded by their friends the Indians.

Rebuilding of the fort began, and the name was changed to Fort Pitt to honor the prime minister of Britain. The place is now Pittsburgh. The tide of the war had changed.

CHAPTER 5

The year 1759 started with British plans for a three-pronged attack on the French. Major General Jeffrey Amherst would take Fort Carillon and then join Major General James Wolfe, who would lead a siege of Quebec. The British also planned to take Fort Niagara and the forts to the west between there and Fort Pitt.

In March, Rogers—now a major—and his rangers scouted out the French strength at Forts Carillon and Crown Point on Lake Champlain. Over the spring and summer, Amherst worked to improve the road from Fort Edward and to build a new fort to replace Fort William Henry. To avoid another panic as in the previous year's attempt on Fort Carillon, Amherst emphasized marksmanship and discipline. In his orderly book, Major John Hawks wrote:

THE DECISIVE BATTLE OF QUEBEC

[O]fficers of Companys take particular care that their men keep their arms in good order and see that their flints are fast in their locks …Whosoever is found guilty of making any disturbance in Camp or Stockade after retreat beating, either by

Jeffrey Amherst (1717–1797) endured an undistinguished military career in Britain until he was called upon to play a major part in the French and Indian War. His success made him a hero, and he went on to become governor of Virginia before returning to England. Some experts believe that Amherst was responsible for spreading the smallpox disease to Native Americans by sending them infected blankets and handkerchiefs, an early form of biological warfare. The oil portrait of Amherst shown above was painted by Sir Joshua Reynolds circa 1768 and is now housed at Yale University.

singing or swearing, or any other noise whereby the guard may be disturbed … they will be severely punished.

The British Control Lake Champlain

In late July, Amherst led 6,000 troops to Fort Carillon, where the number of troops swelled to 11,000. The superior British numbers caused the French to withdraw, but not before they destroyed the fortifications. The French also abandoned Crown Point, leaving Lake Champlain in the hands of the British. The British rebuilt Fort Carillon and renamed it Fort Ticonderoga.

To the west, Fort Niagara also fell without a major battle. One thousand British troops, along with a large contingent of Indians under the command of William Johnson, built trenches a half mile from the fort in early July. French efforts to persuade the Indians to join them failed. The 500 French defending the fort called for reinforcements, but the British ambushed the relief party. On July 25, 1759, the fort commander surrendered. When the French holding forts farther west heard this news, they burned their fortifications and fell back to Detroit.

The stage was now set for the major and defining battle of the French and Indian War, the Battle of Quebec.

British Preparations for Quebec

At the end of April, a British fleet met Major General Wolfe and his 9,000 troops at the mouth of the Saint Lawrence River near Louisbourg. Twenty-two warships and 119 transports sailed up the river. On June 26, they anchored off the Ile d'Orleans, just below Quebec. Countering this force were Montcalm's 16,000 regulars (army troops), colonials, and Indians.

This engraving shows the taking of Quebec. This victory was a turning point in the French and Indian War, allowing England to take most of North America, the rest of which would come later. It was the largest battle of the war, using a force of about 9,000 soldiers and a fleet of 20 ships.

For the next two months, the British built batteries and solidified their position. Both the French and the British engaged in skirmishes, but neither was able to dislodge the other. Wolfe expressed his frustration in a letter to his mother:

My antagonist has wisely shut himself up in inaccessible entrenchments, so that I can't get at him without spilling a

Before deciding to attack Quebec, General Wolfe issued a manifesto (public declaration of principles) to the city's people. It read, in part: "On one side behold England (whose Sincerity is well known) offering them their Effects, and indulging them in every Privilege: On the other side, behold France, inert, and incapable, abandoning them in the most critical Conjuncture." (From the *Boston-Gazette and Country Journal*, May 14, 1759.) When the people of Quebec rejected Wolfe's offer, the city was attacked.

torrent of blood, and that perhaps to no purpose. The Marquis de Montcalm is at the head of a great number of bad soldiers, and I am at the head of a small number of good ones.

By September the British were anxious to get on with the attack on the city. The river below the city was too well guarded to attack from there. Upriver from the city, a sheer 180-foot cliff, l'Anse au Foulon, rose from the water to the flat Plains of Abraham to the north of Quebec. The French assumed that this cliff could not be scaled, so they left it guarded by a token garrison of 100 men.

The account now goes back to Captain Robert Stobo, who had been taken as a hostage by the French when Washington surrendered Fort Necessity in 1754. While being held at Fort

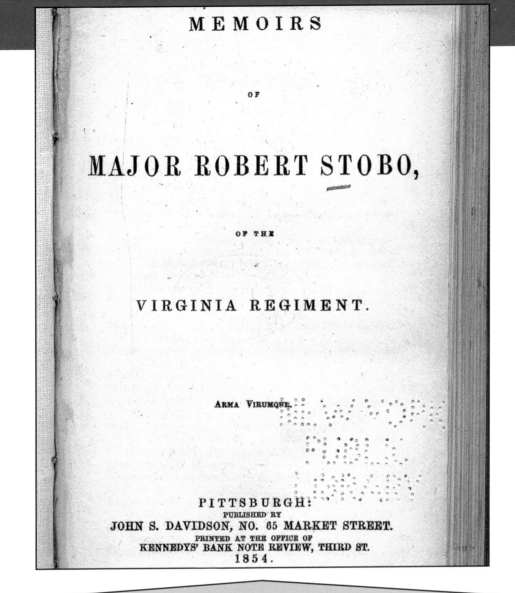

MEMOIRS

OF

MAJOR ROBERT STOBO,

OF THE

VIRGINIA REGIMENT.

ARMA VIRUMQUE.

PITTSBURGH:
PUBLISHED BY
JOHN S. DAVIDSON, NO. 65 MARKET STREET.
PRINTED AT THE OFFICE OF
KENNEDYS' BANK NOTE REVIEW, THIRD ST.
1854.

This is the title page of *Memoirs of Major Robert Stobo of the Virginia Regiment*, published in 1854 by John S. Davidson in Pittsburgh, Pennsylvania. A first edition was printed in London in 1800. When Stobo was captured by the French and imprisoned in Fort Duquesne in 1754, he turned his hostage status into an advantage. His map of the fort helped the British take Quebec.

Duquesne, he had smuggled a sketch of the defense of the fort to Braddock. After discovering this, the French moved Stobo to Quebec. Stobo managed to escape on May 1, 1759. He joined Wolfe's troops and may have conveyed the crucial information that a footpath existed up the l'Anse au Foulon.

British Tactics

On September 12, the British fleet began a bombardment of the main French force at Beauport, just downriver from the city. The maneuver was only a distraction to make the French believe that the British planned to attack there. While the British fleet occupied the French throughout the night, 4,800 British troops landed at the base of l'Anse au Foulon. The first group up the cliff spoke to the guards in French, pretending that they were a reserve force. The sentries relaxed and were captured. Within three hours, all the troops had reached the top.

As dawn approached, the British formed up in ranks on the Plains of Abraham and marched to the walls of Quebec. The main group of 3,000 men marched two deep and one yard apart. They were protected by other troops on their sides and on the rear.

The maneuver stunned Montcalm. After a long night at Beauport waiting for the British attack that never came, he returned to the sight of a long red line stretching across the field. Montcalm didn't wait for reinforcements but began to position his 5,000 troops. At ten in the morning, the French advanced on the British. The British had loaded two balls into each of their muskets. With amazing discipline, they held their fire until the French were within forty yards. As one captain described it: "They delivered as close and heavy a discharge, as I ever saw performed at a private field of exercise . . . and, indeed, well might the French Officers say, that they never opposed such a shock as they received from the center of our line . . . such regularity and discipline they had not experienced before."

The assault was later described by Sir John Fortescue (1859–1933), the historian of the British army, as "the most

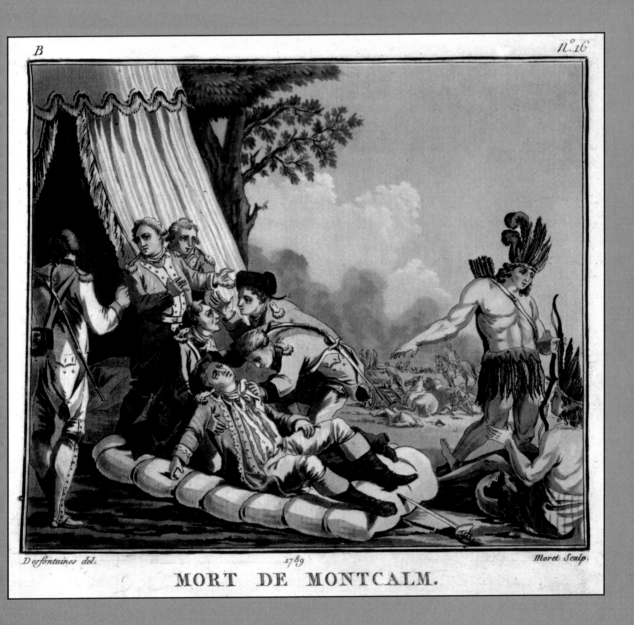

B   n°.16

Desfontaines del.   1789   Moret Sculp.

MORT DE MONTCALM.

This lithograph, *Mort de Montcalm*, was created by Jacques Francois Joseph Swebach using the 1789 engraving *Death of Louis Joseph de Montcalm (1712–1759) at the Siege of Quebec (1759)* by Jean Baptiste Morret. A highly successful military man, Montcalm's image was somewhat sullied by his final defeat to James Wolfe, who also died, on the Plains of Abraham. When the French general learned he would not survive his mortal wounding, he reportedly exclaimed, "Thank God! I shall not live to see the surrender of Quebec."

perfect volley ever fired on a battlefield." After a second round, the French turned and fled.

The main battle lasted only fifteen minutes. Six hundred fifty British troops were killed or wounded, while the French lost 1,500. Both Wolfe and Montcalm lost their lives. The French surrendered Quebec on September 18. The British occupied the city while the French retreated to Montreal, the only place they now held in Canada.

Solidifying the Conquest

Although the Battle of Quebec ended any hopes of French domination in North America, the British knew that France would try to retake the city. Quebec had been ravaged by the British siege, and the British troops there were short on provisions. The men fell victim to illness and overwork as they tried to improve the city's defenses. By the end of the winter, only about 3,000 men were fit for fighting.

On April 20, 1760, General de Levis left Montreal with a force of 6,000 French troops. A week later, the British met the French for a second time on the Plains of Abraham, but this time in reverse, with the British next to the city. The French forced the British back to the walls of the city, but the British held off the attackers until reinforcements and supplies arrived on May 17. The British ships destroyed the French fleet, including the stores and provisions.

To completely eliminate the French threat, the British needed to capture Montreal. Throughout May and June, they amassed forces at Fort Oswego, upriver from Montreal. On August 5, 10,000 British troops and 700 Indians embarked for Montreal. They were joined by two other forces coming from the east and the south. The Montreal defenders saw that any retaliation would be futile and signed the articles of capitulation on September 8, 1760. A week later, Major Rogers captured Fort Detroit for the British, effectively driving the French from North America.

The Last Confrontation

The Indians presented one last lingering problem. In South Carolina, the Cherokee continued to attack settlements despite a treaty they had signed at the end of 1759. This was because the South Carolinians continually pushed past the borders established with the Cherokee. Not until 1761 did the Cherokee stop their raids. As a result of this uprising, Amherst instituted a new policy opposing giving gifts to the Indians. This policy was at odds with that of Johnson, who felt that gift-giving was a method of retaining the friendship of the Indians.

Amherst wrote to Johnson:

> You are sensible how averse I am, to purchasing the good behavior of Indians . . . I think it much better to avoid all presents in future, since that will oblige them to Supply themselves by barter, & of course keep them more Constantly Employed by means of which they will have less time to concert, or Carry in to Execution any Schemes prejudicial to his Majestys Interests.

In April 1763, several tribes tried to regain control of the Ohio Valley. Under the leadership of Pontiac, chief of the Ottawas, they attacked settlers and occupied many of the forts. As the British went after them, the Indians lost many of their chiefs and failed to win any significant victories. Gradually, they lost interest in fighting, and Pontiac capitulated on October 31, 1763. Other

THE
Definitive Treaty
OF
PEACE and FRIENDSHIP,

BETWEEN

His *Britannick* Majesty, the Most
Christian King, and the King of *Spain*.

Concluded at *Paris*, the 10th Day of *February*, 1763.

To which,

The King of *Portugal* acceded on the same Day.

Published by Authority.

LONDON:
Printed by E. OWEN and T. HARRISON, in *Warwick-Lane.* 1763.

The title page of the Treaty of Paris, 1763. See page 57 for an excerpted transcription. The 1763 Treaty of Paris marked the end of the French and Indian War. It was signed in Paris on February 10, 1763, by representatives of England, France, and Spain. All sides agreed that England would control North America east of the Mississippi River, as well as Florida and Louisiana, except for the city of New Orleans. Printed in London by E. Owen and T. Harrison.

tribes gave up the fight, and by November 1764, the majority of Indian tribes had signed peace treaties with the British.

On February 10, 1763, Britain, Spain, and France signed the Treaty of Paris at Versailles, France. All lands east of the Mississippi went to England. All lands west of the Mississippi went to Spain. In addition, France was given New Orleans in exchange for letting Britain have Florida. France kept two islands in the Gulf of Saint Lawrence for fishermen and was allowed to keep Martinique, Guadeloupe, and Saint Lucia in the Caribbean.

The French and Indian War resulted in a new map of North America and set the stage for British dominance. This dominance, however, would last for less than two decades, when the American Revolution changed the map once again.

PRIMARY SOURCE TRANSCRIPTIONS

Page 18: Capitulation at Fort Necessity

Transcription

Capitulation granted by Mons. De Villier, Captain of infantry and commander of troops of his most Christian Majesty, to those English troops actually in the fort of Necessity which was built on the lands of the King's dominions

July the 3rd, at eight o'clock at night, 1754.

As our intention had never been to trouble the peace and good harmony which reigns between the two friendly princes, but only to revenge the assassination which has been done on one of our officers, bearer of a summons, upon his party, as also to hinder any establishment on the lands of the dominions of the King, my master.

Upon these considerations, we are willing to grant protection of favor, to all the English that are in the said fort, upon conditions hereafter mentioned.

Article 1

We grant the English commander to retire with all garrisons, to return peaceably into his own country, and we promise to hinder his receiving any insult from us French, and to restrain as much as shall be in our power the Savages that are with us.

Article 2

He shall be permitted to withdraw and to take with him whatever belongs to them except the artillery, which we reserve for ourselves.

Article 3

We grant them the honors of war; they shall come out with drums beating, and with a small piece of cannon, wishing to show by this means that we treat them as friends.

Article 4

As soon as these Articles are signed by both parties they shall take down the English flag.

Article 5

Tomorrow at daybreak a detachment of French shall receive the surrender of the garrison and take possession of the aforesaid fort.

Article 6

Since the English have scarcely any horses or oxen lift, they shall be allowed to hide their property, in order that they may return to seek for it after they shall have recovered their horses; for this purpose they shall be permitted to leave such number of troops as guards as they may think proper, under this condition that they give their word of honor that they will work on no establishment either in the surrounding country or beyond the Highlands during on year beginning from this day.

Article 7

Since the English have in their power an officer and two cadets, and, in general all the prisoners whom they took when assassinated Sieur de Jumonville they now promise to send them with an escort to Fort Duquesne, situated on Belle River, and to secure the safe performance of this treaty article, as was as of the treaty, Messrs. Jacob Van Braam and Robert Stobo, both Captains shall be delivered to us as hostages until the arrival of our French and Canadians herein before mentioned.

We on our part declare that we shall give an escort to send back in safety the two officers who promise us our French in two months and a half at the latest.

Made out in duplicate on one of the posts of our block-house the same day and year as before.

James Mackay

George Washington

Coulon de Villiers

Page 54: Treaty of Paris, 1763

Transcription

LEWIS, by the grace of God, King of France and Navarre, To all who shall see these presents, Greeting. Whereas the Preliminaries, signed at Fontainebleau the third of November of the last year, laid the foundation of the peace re-established between us and our most dear and most beloved good Brother and Cousin the King of Spain, on the one part, and our most dear and most beloved good Brother the King of Great Britain, and our most dear and most beloved good Brother and Cousin the King of Portugal on the other, We have had nothing more at heart since that happy epoch, than to consolidate and strengthen in the most lasting manner, so salutary and so important a work, by a solemn and definitive treaty between Us and the said powers. For these causes, and other good considerations, Us thereunto moving, We, trusting entirely in the capacity and experience, zeal and fidelity for our service, of our most dear and well-beloved Cousin, Csar Gabriel de Choiseul, Duke of Praslin, Peer of France, Knight of our Orders, Lieutenant General of our Forces and of the province of Britany, Counsellor in all our Councils, Minister and Secretary of State, and of our Commands and Finances, . . . In witness whereof, we have caused our Seal to be put to these presents. Given at Versailles the 7th day of the month of February, in the year of Grace 1763, and of our reign the forty-eighth. Signed Lewis, and on the fold, by the King, the Duke of Choiseul. Sealed with the great Seal of yellow Wax.

# GLOSSARY

artillery Weapons that are mounted on a carriage or that are used for discharging missiles such as catapults.

bateau A flat-bottomed rowboat.

besiege To surround with armed forces for the purpose of forcing surrender.

blockade Cutting off trade, communications, and supplies from the enemy.

breach To make a hole in a fortification.

breastwork A temporary fortification or addition to an existing fortification.

capitulation Agreement to terms of surrender.

commission The authority to perform certain duties.

diplomacy The art of negotiations between nations.

encroach To gradually enter into the territory of another.

entourage Attendants who go with another person.

garrison Troops stationed at a military post.

grievance A complaint regarding unfair treatment.

magazine The building in which ammunition and explosives are stored at a military installation.

militiamen Able-bodied men who are in military service.

orderly book The journal in which military orders were entered.

parapet A wall of earth or stone built to protect soldiers.

plunder To take goods by force.

portage To transport.

provincials Soldiers paid by their own colonies, who enlisted for specific campaigns, for terms of service no longer than a year.

scurvy A disease caused by a lack of ascorbic acid. This was common among sailors and others who were not able to get fresh fruit to eat.

skirmish A minor battle, usually between a small group of isolated troops.

speculators People who engage in risky business transactions with the hope of making a profit.

stockade A line of timbers set into the ground in a way to make a defensive fortification.

victuals Food.

FOR MORE INFORMATION

Fort Edwards Foundation
P.O. Box 623
Capon Bridge, WV 26711
(304) 822-4655
Web site: http://www.fortedwards.org

Fort Pitt Museum
101 Commonwealth Place
Point State Park
Pittsburgh, PA 15222
(412) 281-9284
Web site: http://www.fortpittmuseum.com

Fort Ticonderoga
P.O. Box 390
Ticonderoga, NY 12883
(518) 585-2821
Web site: http://www.fort-ticonderoga.org

Web Sites

Due to the changing nature of Internet links, the Rosen Publishing
Group, Inc., has developed an online list of Web sites related to the sub-
ject of this book. This site is updated regularly. Please use this link to
access the list:

http://www.rosenlinks.com/psah/friw

# FOR FURTHER READING

Chidsey, Donald Barr. *The French and Indian War*. New York: Crown, 1969.

Cuneo, John. *Robert Rogers of the Rangers*. New York: Richardson and Steirman, 1987.

Mann, Albert. *Struggle for a Continent*. New York: Atheneum, 1987.

O'Meara, Walter. *Guns at the Forks*. Englewood Cliffs, NJ: Prentice-Hall, 1965.

Schwartz, Seymour. *The French and Indian War, 1754–1763: The Imperial Struggle For North America*. New York: Simon & Schuster, 1994.

Williams, Noel St. John. *Redcoats Along the Hudson*. Herndon, VA: Brassey's, 1997.

BIBLIOGRAPHY

Anderson, Fred. *Crucible of War: The Seven Years' War and the Fate of Empire in British North America, 1754–1766*. New York: Alfred A. Knopf, 2000.

Cuneo, John. *Robert Rogers of the Rangers*. New York: Richardson and Steirman, 1987.

Downes, Randolph C. *Council Fires on the Upper Ohio*. Pittsburgh: University of Pittsburgh Press, 1940.

Hamilton, Edward P. *The French and Indian Wars: The Story of Battles and Forts in the Wilderness*. New York: Doubleday & Company, 1962.

Jennings, Francis. *Empire of Fortune: Crowns, Colonies and Tribes in the Seven Years War in America*. New York: W.W. Norton & Company, 1988.

Kopperman, Paul E. *Braddock at the Monongahela*. Pittsburgh: University of Pittsburgh Press, 1977.

Nester, William R. *The Great Frontier War: Britain, France, and the Imperial Struggle for North America, 1607–1755*. Westport, CT: Praeger, 2000.

Parkman, Francis. *Montcalm and Wolfe: The Riveting Story of the Heroes of the French and Indian War*. New York: AMS Press, 1969.

Schwartz, Seymour. *The French and Indian War, 1754–1763: The Imperial Struggle For North America*. New York: Simon & Schuster, 1994.

PRIMARY SOURCE IMAGE LIST

Page 5: Map of Ohio, New England, New York, New Jersey, Pennsylvania, Maryland, Virginia, and the Carolinas. Created by Gilles Robert de Vaugondy in 1755. Hand colored. Housed in the Library of Congress Geography and Map Division in Washington, D.C.

Page 11: *Washington as Colonel of the Virginia Regiment*. Oil on canvas portrait of Colonel George Washington. Painted by Charles Willson Peale in 1772. From the Washington/Custis/Lee Collection at Washington and Lee University, Lexington, Virginia.

Page 14: A plan of Fort Duquesne as it appeared in 1754. From a broadside, London, England, by J. Payne in 1756. Housed in the Library of Congress in Washington, D.C.

Page 16: Woodcut cartoon, "Join, or Die." Created by Benjamin Franklin in 1754. From the Library of Congress in Washington, D.C.

Page 18: Capitulation at Fort Necessity. Signed on July 3, 1754. Housed in the Royal Ontario Museum in Toronto, Canada.

Page 23: Sketch of Edward Braddock's advance party. By Orme. From the William L. Clements Library at the University of Michigan.

Page 26: *Defeat of General Braddock, in the French and Indian War, in Virginia, in 1755.* Engraving circa 1855. Housed in the Library of Congress.

Page 29: *A South View of Oswego, on Lake Ontario, in North America.* Engraved for *London Magazine*, 1760s. From the National Archives of Canada.

Page 31: Portrait of Robert Rogers. Based on the 1776 engraving by Thomas Hart.

Page 33: Painting of a ranger at work near the lines at Lake George. Created by Thomas Davies in 1759.

Page 35: Illustration of the scalping of English prisoners. From *The Cruel Massacre of the Protestants in North-America: Shewing How the French and Indians Joined Together to Scalp the English, and the Manner of their Scalping*, 1761. Published in London, England.

Page 41: Portrait of Viscount George Augustus Howe. Oil on canvas. Painted by Sir Joshua Reynolds in the eighteenth century. Housed at Christie's images in London.

Page 45: Portrait of Sir Jeffrey Amherst. Oil on canvas. Painted by Sir Joshua Reynolds circa 1768. Housed in the Paul Mellon Collection, Yale Center for British Art in New Haven, Connecticut.

Page 47: *A View of the Taking of Quebec, September 13th 1759.* Eighteenth-century engraving by an artist from the English School. From a private collection.

Page 48: Portrait of General Wolfe (1727–1759). Oil on canvas. Painted by J. S. C. Schaak in the eighteenth century. From a private collection.

Page 49: Title page of *Memoirs of Major Robert Stobo of the Virginia Regiment*. Published in 1854 by John S. Davidson in Pittsburgh, Pennsylvania.

Page 51: *Death of Louis Joseph de Montcalm (1712–1759) at the Siege of Quebec (1759)* engraving by Jean Baptiste Morret in 1789. Colored lithograph *Mort de Montcalm* by Jacques Francois Joseph Swebach. From a private collection.

Page 54: Title page of the 1763 Treaty of Paris. Signed on February 10, 1763. Printed in London by E. Owen and T. Harrison. Housed in the New York Public Library.

INDEX

About the Author

Carolyn Gard is a writer who lives in Boulder, Colorado. When she's not writing, she enjoys hiking in the mountains with her two German shepherds. She has written many books for Rosen Publishing, including one about the September 11 attacks on the World Trade Center and the Pentagon.

Photo Credits

Cover, pp. 1, 21 © Hulton Archive/Getty Images; pp. 5, 14, 38 Library of Congress, Geography and Map Division; p. 11 Washington-Custis-Lee Collection, Washington and Lee University; p. 16 Library of Congress, Prints and Photographs Division; p. 18 Royal Ontario Museum, Toronto; pp. 23, 35 William T. Clements Library, University of Michigan; p. 26 Library of Congress/Bridgeman Art Library; p. 29 National Archives of Canada, C-9418/Canadian Heritage Gallery; p. 31 © Bettmann/CORBIS; p. 33 Collections of the Fort Ticonderoga Museum; p. 41 © Christie's Images, Ltd.; p. 45 © Yale Center for British Art, Paul Mellon Collection, USA/Bridgeman Art Library; p. 47 private collection/Bridgeman Art Library; p. 48 private collection/Phillips, The International Fine Art Auctioneers/Bridgeman Art Library; p. 49 General Research Division, The New York Public Library, Astor, Lenox and Tilden Foundations; p. 51 Private Collection/The Stapleton Collection/Bridgeman Art Library; p. 54 Rare Books and Manuscripts Collection, New York Public Library, Astor, Lenox and Tilden Foundations.

Designer: Nelson Sá; Editor: Christine Poolos; Photo Researcher: Peter Tomlinson

L
1/04

973.2 jG c.1
Gard, Carolyn.
The French and Indian War